AF578779

The Dragon Hunter's Handbook

JOYCE HARGREAVES

Illustrated by the author
Maps by Brian Hargreaves

GRANADA
London Toronto Sydney New York

Published by Granada Publishing 1983
Granada Publishing Limited
Frogmore, St Albans, Herts AL2 2NF
and
36 Golden Square, London W1R 4AH
515 Madison Avenue, New York, NY 10022, USA
117 York Street, Sydney, NSW 2000, Australia
60 International Blvd, Rexdale, Ontario, R9W 6J2, Canada
61 Beach Road, Auckland, New Zealand

British Library Cataloguing in Publication Data
Hargreaves, Joyce
The dragon hunter's handbook.
1. Dragons – Juvenile literature
I. Title
398'.469 GR830.D7

ISBN 0 246 12226 9

Printed in Great Britain by
William Clowes (Beccles) Ltd,
Beccles and London

Contents

1 The Shape of the Dragon 4

2 Fact or Fiction? 14

3 'Here be Dragons' 24

4 The Gurt Vurm of Shervage Wood 34

5 The Battle of the Barrel 42

6 Dragon's Retreat 50

7 The Laidly Worm of Spindlestone Heugh 58

8 Merlin and the Fighting Dragons 68

9 The Wells of the Invisible Dragon 76

10 The Wyvern of Cynwch Lake 84

11 The Legend of Nine Tempting Maidens 92

12 Who Was St George? 100

Book list 109

1
The Shape of the Dragon

DRAGON HUNTING is not like any known type of nature watching. You cannot search for a dragon underneath a hedgerow or in the zoo, it is not even a creature that is mentioned in modern books of natural history. A very different type of detection work is required. You have to delve into the past, look at ancient sculptures and carvings, read the legends of the countryside and be able to interpret the meanings of the names of places and sites of antiquity.

The dragon is the most famous, most feared and possibly the oldest of legendary beasts but what does it look like? Only pictures in words, and on parchment and stone can tell us. The Oxford Dictionary describes the dragon as a mythical monster like a crocodile or snake who breathes fire and has wings and claws. It is also said to be a sea creature or serpent.

This seems rather confusing but if we trace the dragon's history back to earlier times the reason why it is described in so many different ways becomes clearer. Dragon and serpent are often names used for the same creature. The oldest known drawings of dragons in the British Isles show them looking like a snake or serpent. This reptile was called an 'orme' or more familiarly a 'worm', names derived from the Norse word *ormr* which means dragon.

The name orme or worm was absorbed into the English language after Norsemen invaded

parts of Britain during the eighth and ninth centuries A.D. Among the stories and legends that they brought with them was the legend of the Midgard Worm. This creature slept in the sea, its tail in its mouth, and surrounded the whole world with the coils of its body. It was said that, should the tail ever be removed, disaster would follow.

The Worm was nothing like the resplendent, four legged beast that is pictured in books, films and heraldry today. It lacked the glamour of flashing claws and gleaming scales and was described as a great goggly eyed, slimy serpent with foul breath, uglier even than a leech. It was portrayed in carvings and manuscripts with a reptilian or horselike head at one end of a completely serpentine body. Examples of this type of dragon can be seen in the illustrations of St George killing the dragon in Chapter 12.

Some of the dragons that were shown in the Celtic designs of a later date showed a change of shape. These creatures were transformed into fiercer beasts who were more dramatic adversaries of the dragon-killing heroes than the nondescript Worm. They were shown with a savage head on a snake's long body, two legs and a pair of wings ribbed like those of a bat. This bipedal (two legged) creature is known as a Wyvern, a name that comes from the French word *vivere*, meaning viper. The Wyvern is often seen in heraldry where it is the symbol of war and pestilence.

By the end of the twelfth century artists added

An Amphisbaena from a piece of embroidery

yet another type of dragon to their collection of decorative beasts, making it into an even more destructive creature. Although it now lacked the doomladen mystery of the Worm, this dragon

A Hydra. 14th century painting

was changed into an even bolder fighter. It still retained the fierce head, wings and forelegs of the Wyvern and the long body and flexible tail of the serpent. Now sharp teeth and claws and two more legs had been added to make it still more dangerous. It could also breath out smoke and flames. This portrait describes the elegant and sometimes sinister dragon that is familiar to us today.

There are a number of dragons which are illustrated with an extra head at the end of their tails. Pictures of St Michael and St George show them fighting dragons of this type. Two-headed dragons are called Amphisbaenas. They usually have a problem in knowing which way to move as they can run just as fast in both directions, being guided first by one head and then by the other.

A many-headed beast of the dragon family is called a Hydra. The Hydra is portrayed either with a snake's or a wyvern's body. In the Bible it is described as 'a great red dragon, having seven heads and ten horns and seven crowns upon his heads'. The Hydra that was killed by Heracles in the Greek myths had up to a hundred heads and whenever one of its heads was chopped off another two or three grew in its place. As its name suggests, the Hydra lived in or near water.

The Worm is also said to make its home in or near water, by the sides of rivers or lakes, in wells or even in the sea. It is for this reason that the sea serpent and the lake monster can also be regarded as belonging to the dragon family. The Sea Dragon can vary in form from a sea serpent, a long thin creature like a snake, to an inhabitant of the deep whose shape and size resemble those of a whale.

A sea Dragon from a book of Sea Monsters

There are two types of river or lake monsters. One has a head similar to that of a horse and is called in Scotland the Highland Water Horse or Kelpie and in Wales the Ceffyl Dwr.

The other lake monster is called a Pieste and is similar to the horse-headed dragons but instead of an equine head this creature has one that is flat and serpentine. Probably the most famous beast of this type is the Loch Ness Monster.

There are a number of other members of the dragon family that can also trace their ancestry back to the Worm. The first of these is the Basilisk which is considered to be king of the snakes, the absolute monarch of smaller reptiles, as the dragon is the king of larger reptiles. Although it is less than three feet long it is said to be as savage as the most destructive of dragons.

The Basilisk lived in the desert, in fact it was the cause of the desert, for the breath of this venomous beast was so destructive that it could wither all the surrounding vegetation and even set fire to the stones. The smell of its sweat was enough to destroy any living being and the water of the streams where it drank became poisonous. The creature could also spit its venom into the air and any bird flying past would be frazzled by the monster's poison and fall dead to the ground.

The most lethal weapon in the Basilisk's armory was its glowing eyes. One searing glance from its eyes was enough to kill a man instantly. (There is an expression, still in use today, that describes an intent and hard look as a 'basilisk stare'.) Fortunately for its potential victims, this murderous look was also the Basilisk's downfall for the sight of its own reflected eyes in a mirror was enough to kill the Basilisk itself.

A Basilisk from a 13th century bestiary

It was reported that the deserts of North Africa were infested with Basilisks and travellers crossing the desert used to take a cockerel with them as protection. This was because the crowing of an ordinary cock sent the Basilisk into a fit from which it never recovered.

At first the Basilisk was portrayed as a serpent with a crest upon its head but like the dragon it too acquired a shape more in keeping with its regal and horrific reputation. In medieval times, when Basilisks were said to be the scourge of Europe, a Basilisk would be illustrated with a thicker, heavier body supported by up to eight legs and its serpentine head wore a crown. This is a reminder that the Basilisk is a royal creature. A particularly savage Basilisk from Saxony was described as very fat with a speckled white body, a blue back and a coiled tail.

The Cockatrice is closely linked to the Basilisk. The travellers in Africa who took a cock with them as protection began describing a new and different type of Basilisk, one that had the head of a cock instead of the narrow one of a serpent. This creature was first described as a Basilcock and later as a Cockatrice.

The Cockatrice was just as savage as the Basilisk and it had a very curious history. The creature had to be born from a toughened shell-less egg laid by a seven year old cock during the time that Sirius, the dog star, could be seen. The egg was to be spherical not ovoid and had to be hatched out by a toad or a snake upon a dung heap. The winged Cockatrice that sprang forth from this egg had the head and body of a cock and always had a coiled Wyvern's tail. Its eyes still retained the murderous stare of a Basilisk and looked like those of a toad. The body and tail were both yellow and sometimes the tail had an extra head on its tip which was just as poisonous as the main head. There are some legends about the Cockatrice in England. The most well known recounts the story of the Wherwell Cockatrice.

Stonecarving of Ceres and her serpent/dragons

2
FACT OR FICTION?

IN MANY STORIES the plot, location and characters are completely fictional. A legend is different because it has a basis of fact that can be exaggerated, condensed or gradually changed, over a period of time, so that its original meaning is lost. In this book all the tales about dragons are legends and are, at least, partly true.

In the legends retold in the following chapters, the places mentioned actually exist and can be visited. At the time that they were chronicled, it is likely that there was something strange or unusual happening in the countryside. Something worth recording in the form of a sensational story.

What were these unusual events? Did a dragon actually appear and cause havoc in a village or were the culprits a band of robbers carrying a banner with a dragon painted on it? Read on and you will find some of the most likely theories that could account for the appearances of dragons.

If a legend can be a report of an actual happening, however exaggerated, this raises another question. Were there any dragons alive when the legends were told and are any alive today?

The answer must be a qualified 'yes' for, in the reptile section of the Natural History Museum in London, there is a four legged, long tailed creature which is known as a Komodo dragon. It can be found on Komodo and other small islands off the coast of Indonesia. The reason why it cannot be regarded as the true dragon of myth and legend is because of the location in which it is found. A creature known in such a small area could not have been responsible for the great quantity of dragon folklore than can be read today.

Other creatures that resemble our modern interpretations of dragons are certain types of prehistoric monsters. It has been suggested that race memories of primitive creatures like the Pterodactylus, known as the flying dragon, might account for the legends but it seems unlikely that men and prehistoric beasts ever encountered each other. Prehistoric monsters are supposed to have only existed before man appeared on the earth. However, it is known that fossilized bones of some of these creatures were unearthed in medieval times. It seems more likely that the four legged dragon that was portrayed in the carvings and manuscripts of the

A Dinosaur

Middle Ages was actually based on the skeletons of prehistoric monsters.

Some legends record that the dragon lived in a lake or in the sea and it could be that some species of creature, descended from prehistoric monsters, do still exist either in the ocean or in deep lakes. One example of such a creature that may yet survive is the Loch Ness Monster. There have been a number of expeditions by scientists and other interested people to Loch Ness to try and find out if there is a monster in the lake. As yet there have been no definite results one way or the other. Perhaps one day we will know for certain whether 'Nessie' lives or not!

There are only a limited number of dragon legends that could be said to be based on living animals. This does not mean that all the other dragons mentioned in legends are completely fanciful. For a start the dragon, in its snakelike form, is an ancient religious symbol. Many hundreds of years ago the serpent and the dragon were regarded as the same creature. Long before the word 'Worm' was used in Britain to represent a serpentine form of dragon, the names *drakon* and *draco* were used throughout the Greek and Roman empires to describe a large snake. The word dragon is derived from both of these names.

From the beginning of our civilization people worshipped the Earth Goddess. She was one of the most important deities for she controlled the fertility of the land. Pictures of the goddess usually show her with a serpent guardian which was the symbol of her power over the elemental forces which could be either savage or beneficial. The goddess was known by many names. The most familiar to us is her Roman one of Ceres. Ceres had a chariot drawn by dragons and she is portrayed holding her serpent dragons and other emblems of fertility to show her association with the growing powers and energies of the earth. She was not the only Roman deity who was depicted with a dragon. It is shown, in serpent form, on the shield of Minerva, the Goddess of Learning, where it is the sign of her wisdom.

The dragon Ladon guarded the apples on the tree of the Hesperides for the goddess Juno. Ladon was the obvious choice for this job as dragons are reputed to have excellent eyesight. When Ladon was defeated by the hero Hercules, Juno placed him in the sky as the constellation

Serpens under the care of the serpent holder Ascelapius, the God of Healing. Ascelapius carries Ladon, his curative serpent, coiled about his staff. Mercury also carries serpents, two of them coiled about a wand. The wand and serpents together are known as a cadeucus which is also a symbol of healing and one that is still used today by the medical profession.

Another religion that originated in Italy and was well known in Roman Britain was the worship of the horned god Cernunnos. Pictures of Cernunnos show him accompanied by his ram headed serpent, a dragon with horns on its head. Cernunnos was the Lord of the Underworld and was responsible for health, wealth and commerce. His dragon too is associated with wealth, especially that which is found underground.

When the Romans invaded Britain they built temples to their gods and goddesses here to join, or oust, the other pagan religions that already existed. In time these religious beliefs (which included the worship of the divine serpent) would have been incorporated into the legends of the country. This probably accounts for a number of legends about dragons guarding hidden gold, healing waters or maidens.

When a new religion conquers the old established customs, the gods of the old religion are either incorporated into the new one or are turned into demons. This is why in Christian times the dragon is regarded as totally evil. When Christianity became the dominant religion in Britain, the serpent/dragon became sadly changed. The horned god and other fertility deities were combined to become the squatting, horned and hooved Satan, and the serpent of

Dragon as the 'Gate of Hell' from the Winchester Psalter

wisdom and fertility was transformed into the sinful Worm, a fitting companion for the devil. Medieval artists actually drew the Gates of Hell as a dragon's mouth open to receive the damned. The dragon was also portrayed as the evil that saints had to conquer either by the sword or, as in the case of St Margaret, by bursting it apart with her crucifix. Today you can see many pictures of saints and dragons in combat in churches and cathedrals.

Not all British dragons have their origins in memories of factual creatures or in religious symbolism. Some can have more bloodthirsty explanations. The dragon's reputed fierceness has led both soldiers and pirates to use a picture of the dragon as a sign of their courage.

Towns on the coastlines of England and Scotland used to be raided by pillaging Danes who crossed the sea in their longboats. These vessels had elaborately carved figureheads usually in the shape of a dragon's head, put there to strike terror in the hearts of their victims. A pirate raid of this sort could be described in a legend as a dragon who came out of the sea, attacked the town and burnt it with its fiery breath. The story of a brave warrior fighting off the dragon could, in fact, be the story of the town's boldest inhabitants fighting off the raiding Danes.

Armies, both in the past and today, used sculptural and drawn dragons on their banners, heraldic emblems and weapons. In Britain the leader of an army used to be called a Pendragon and even today there is a regiment of soldiers

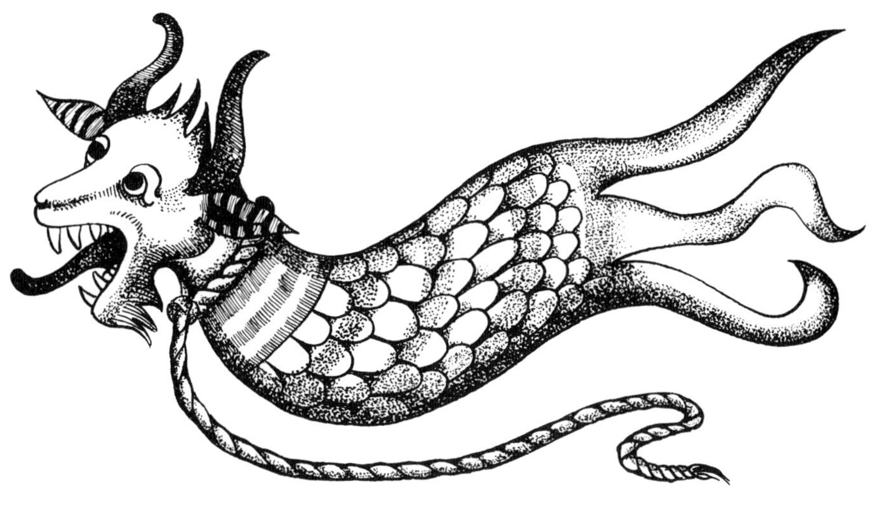

A 15th century windsock dragon

called Dragoon Guards. Draco or windsock banners were a familiar sight in Europe during the latter part of the Roman Empire and were among the chief insignia of the Roman armies. The windsock, held by the standard bearer of the cohort called a Draconarius, consisted of a pole with a carved dragon's head on top of it. A tube of cloth was attached to the head and when the banner was held aloft it filled with air, billowing and writhing like a living creature. The fierce appearance of these banners (and some could look very realistic) had the effect of terrifying the enemy as well as assisting the archers in the army, by showing them in which direction the wind was blowing. In legendary terms, the foes of one of these armies could claim that dragons had attacked them.

Many legends about dragons describe their hot, fiery breath and their ability to fly from place to place. In ancient times men were more preoccupied with the night sky than city dwellers are today. If a comet appeared overhead it could be described as a fiery, swirling, elongated object. It would not stretch the imagination too much to describe it as a dragon. In the *History of the Kings of England,* written in the twelfth century, a comet was said to be 'like a dragon' and in more modern times both Swift's and Holmes's comets were described as flying serpents. The sight of a comet or meteor could therefore go into legend as a story of an evil flaming dragon which caused terror in the hearts of all who saw it.

Any large flying object in the past was likely to have been called a dragon and here is another theory and one that is very recent as it involves visitors from other planets. Could a UFO in ancient times have been described as a dragon? There are a number of people who think that this may be so.

If we look at ancient legends there are a number of occasions when dragons have carried people or gods through the air. Both Ceres and the sorceress Medea had dragon chariots and a Japanese legend recounts an even closer identification of a serpent with a UFO.

The Goddess of Fire and Earth wished to descend to the ground in order to instruct mankind. The Heavenly Serpent, who loved her, offered help. He coiled himself into a spiral around the body of the goddess and swiftly flew down to earth with her. They were accompanied by other serpents coiled into circles and their speedy descent left round depressions in the ground where they landed.

Is the dragon a real creature, a religious symbol, a force for both good and evil, a comet, a UFO or even something else? Nobody knows for certain but remember that the dragon is a magical creature which would probably cover its comings and goings around the countryside with a veil of mystery.

Medea's dragon chariot 4th century A.D.

A Jenny Haniver

3
'HERE BE DRAGONS'

YOU NOW KNOW the different types of dragon, their names and some of the reasons why they are so well known. Now to the main purpose of this book. How do we hunt dragons?

You *could* spend weeks camping on the edge of a lake hoping to see some strange creature arising from its murky depths but it is most unlikely that you would get even a glimpse of a lake monster. The best place to look for dragons is in written legends, in pictures, and in place names and on maps.

There are many legends about dragons in the British Isles. Look at the map on page 25. It shows about half of the places that are associated

Dornoch
Cnoc-na-Cnoimh
Loch Ness
Loch Morar
Strathmartine
Bamburgh
Linton
Dalry
Longwitton
Worm Hill
Handale
Renwick
Sockburn
Slingsby
Wortley
Dinas Emrys
Anwick
Ludham
Llyn Cynwch
Bromfield
Brinsop
St Osyths
Newcastle Emlyn
Dragonhord
Wiston
Mordiford
Bures
White Horse Vale
St Leonards
Forest
Lyminster
Shervage Wood
Wherwell
Winkleigh

with dragons. Wherever you live there should be one or more locations that are near enough for you to visit.

The best way to find out about any one particular dragon is to first read about it in a book. The oldest known version is often the most accurate because anyone who retells the story, including me, will use his or her own imagination to add little details to the original tale. You can sometimes find old books of legends in your local library. If you can't find the book you want, ask the librarian to get it for you. He or she can do this for a small fee.

At the back of this book is a short list of books that may be helpful. Included are some that are mainly picture books and show a great variety of dragons from all over the world.

Some old maps show places reputedly visited by dragons, but take care when looking at them. The words 'here be dragons' or the picture of a dragon often appears on a map but it does not always mean that it was the site of a dragon legend. Cartographers of an earlier age used to make their maps into works of art. They were decorated with drawings of Neptune, zephyrs and other fabulous creatures. It is not unknown for a map maker to fill an unattractive blank space on a map, usually a deserted or desolate place, with the words 'here be dragons' or the picture of a dragon, just to make the map look more decorative.

There is another way of finding out about dragons by using ordnance survey maps. In legends dragons often live coiled around sacred hills, in wells, or they guard ancient barrows. These places often lie on the ancient site alignments that are called ley lines. Leys are found by circling, in pencil, all the ancient sites that you can find on a map. These include old churches, especially those that have their foundations built upon pagan remains, barrows, standing stones

The dragon in this heraldic drawing is not devouring its prey. It represents enlightenment coming out of wisdom.

and circles, castles, traditional wells, etc. If you can draw a straight line through a number of these sites, it is possible that you have found a ley line. *The Ley Hunter's Companion* (details in the book list) will tell you all that you want to know about ley lines. If you find one of these lines on a map there is occasionally a chance that somewhere on the ley there will be a place where there is a legend about a dragon.

Usually it is a story that first makes you want to find out more about any particular dragon but there are other ways of tracking these elusive beasts. The name of a place can give a clue to the existence of a legend about a dragon. The word worm or orm, as was explained in Chapter 1, means dragon and can be found in a number of place names. There is a headland called Great Orms Head in Llandudno and villages called Ormsby (Orms village) in Norfolk and Ormskirk (Orms church) in Lancashire. Do you know any towns called Wormley, Worminford or Wormshill? They could be the sites of a dragon legend. The word drake from *drakon*, the Greek word for dragon (it has no connection with ducks!), can be found in a town called Drakelow in Derbyshire. A dragon, it is said, once lived here. Look out for place names with drake in them. Legends about dragons who guard treasure seem to have a particular connection with these sites.

There is a well known legend about a dragon called 'The Knuckler' who lived in a small lake at Lyminster. There used to be a number of deep pools in Sussex, like this one. They were known

A dragon fighting a centaur from Westminster Abbey

as knuckler holes. Places with nicker, nuckler or knuckler in their names indicate localities where there is deep water either in a pool or in a river bed. Some of these could be associated with a dragon legend because *nicor* is the Anglo-Saxon word for a sea monster.

When you have found the site of a dragon legend it is worth exploring further. Look in the local church first. Christianity has cast the dragon in the role of a villain and it is often shown in church decorations being trampled under the feet of the righteous. Sometimes, in older churches, there are small reminders of its pagan past. Dragons can be seen carved into bench ends, roof bosses and rood screens with grape vines twined about them. In some cases the vine is actually growing out of the dragon's mouth. This shows the dragon in the guise of a fertility spirit which made sure that the earth was always fruitful. The winged serpent, which represents wisdom, can be seen on a cross at Ruthwell in Dumfries. A copy of it is in the Victoria and Albert Museum in London.

Naturally all the churches dedicated to the Archangel Michael who drove the devil, in the shape of a dragon, out of Heaven, to St Margaret who burst the dragon with her cross and to St George, will show a picture of the saint and the dragon somewhere in the building. The places to look for dragons are in stained glass windows, banners and, most important, in carvings. They can also be seen decorating a tympanum in a church. A tympanum is the carved panel set above the lintel of a door.

A church sometimes contains the weapons of a man reputed to be a dragon killer. A spear that is said to be the one that killed the flying dragon of Aller can be seen in the church at nearby Low Ham. The falchion with which Sir John Conyers slew the dragon of Sockburn is in Durham Cathedral. The tombstone of Piers Shonks, another dragon killer, can be seen in Brent Pelham church in Hertfordshire. This tombstone is 700 years old and has a cross carved on it with

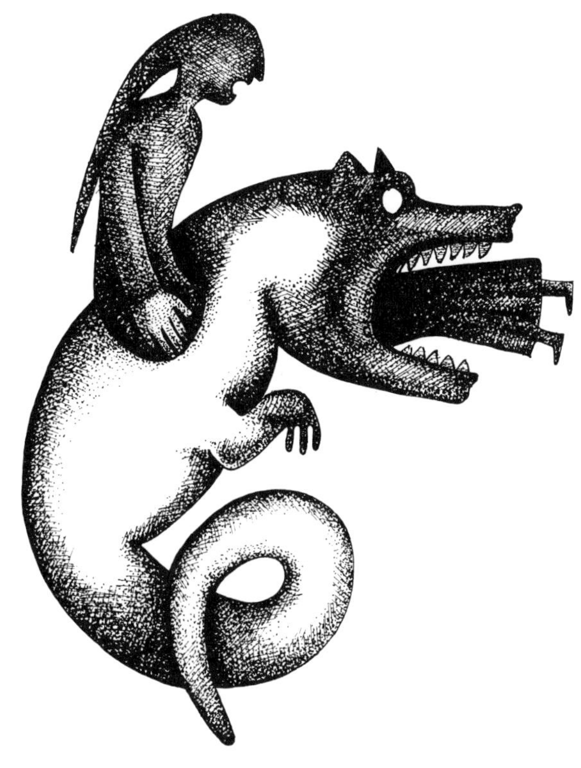

A stonecarving of St Margaret bursting the dragon

the foot of the cross thrust into the open mouth of a dragon.

Try visiting any ancient buildings that are open to the public and near the site of a dragon legend. Look for pictures, carvings and written information about the legend. Generally the owners of castles, abbeys and other historical sites are proud of their dragons. They will display any information or pictures that they have of their very own legendary beast.

Museums can also contain items of interest. Most museums will have some carved or painted dragons. Look especially for the Worm – the serpentine type of dragon – which can be seen in collections of Norse or Celtic artefacts.

You can see a stuffed Komodo dragon in the Natural History Museum in London. But a word of caution here. When looking at stuffed animals in small or private museums, you could see a small creature that is labelled as a dragon. This will not be a dragon at all. It is a fake that is known as a Jenny Haniver. A Jenny Haniver is a creature that has been made from parts of dead fish, chickens and other small animals. A dead fish, usually a skate, is given a dragonish shape by curling its side fins over its back and twisting its tail into coils. The fish is dried and then preserved with a coat of varnish. A Cockatrice was discovered in 1824. The fisherman who brought it to the scientists declared that it had been found alive in the English Channel. It had indeed been found alive in the sea for the body of the creature was a treated fiddle fish with the legs of a cockerel added.

In each of the following nine chapters a dragon legend is retold. The place where the dragon was seen is investigated and the most likely explanations for the legends are included. Sometimes there is a map alongside the story to show the exact positions of the places mentioned. This will help you if you go to see them. The illustrations include sketches of objects that are connected with the legends. These pictures show parts of ancient manuscripts, a woodcarving, a tympanum, a stonecarving from a pagan site, a piece of jewellery and a pictish stone. You will probably be able to find many other fascinating things connected with dragons. Good hunting!

4
The Gurt Vurm of Shervage Wood

ONCE, not so long ago, a gigantic Worm lived in Shervage Wood. It lay coiled in the undergrowth around the bottom of a tree and would only stir itself when it was hungry. Then it would slide quietly out of the wood and make itself a snack of half a dozen local sheep or ponies. It grew so fat that its girth was as thick as that of two ancient oaks joined together.

Soon the farmers who lived nearby began to wonder why there were hardly any cattle to be seen on the hillside around Shervage Wood. There would be no animals to send to Bridgwater Fair that year. The farmers were worried and said to each other, 'Where be they ponies gone to then? Be there a Gurt Vurm up in the wood eating they?' A shepherd and two gipsy horse dealers decided to go up to the wood to see if they could find anything but they were never seen again. After that everyone avoided Shervage Wood. Nobody was even willing to gather the plentiful supplies of bilberries that grew on the hillside there.

Close by the wood, in the town of Crowcombe, there lived an aged crone who was a superb cook. Her speciality was bilberry tarts. She covered each tart with thick cream and her pastry just melted in the mouth. They were delicious! But if nobody would collect the fruit for her, she wouldn't be able to sell her tarts at Triscombe Revel that year and there would be no money to pay her rent. The poor old woman was very upset.

One day a stranger came knocking at her door, a woodman looking for work. This gave the old woman an idea. 'Why don't 'ee do some cutting in Shervage Wood,' she said, 'and at the same time see if they bilberries be ripe.' The old crone was so desperate to get her fruit that she didn't warn him about the Vurm that lurked there. She gave him a jug of ale and some food and sent him up the hill towards the wood.

By the time the woodcutter had climbed the hill into the woods and picked a quantity of bilberries for the old woman, he felt in need of a drink. In the shade, underneath some trees, he spotted a great log lying amongst the ferns. He sat down on it, took a swig of ale and started on his bread and cheese.

Suddenly the log began to wriggle and squirm beneath him. The woodcutter jumped to his feet in alarm. 'Hold a bit,' he yelled, 'thee do move, do thee. Take that then!' And he swung his axe down so hard that he cut the log clean in two. Blood began to run out of both halves of the severed trunk for it was not a log at all but the body of the Gurt Vurm.

Then one half of the Vurm slithered away as fast as it could to Bilbrook and as it was the tail

end, there it promptly died. The people of Bilbrook call this place Dragon Cross. The other end, the one with the head, wriggled off to Kingston St Mary and what happened to it there is another story.

The woodman just sat down and finished his meal, cut his wood and took the old woman as many bilberries as he could carry. 'There were a dragon in that wood,' he told her a trifle suspiciously but all she said was, 'Didn't 'ee know? Didn't someone tell 'ee?'

This is a good legend to use to start hunting dragons because it is easy to find all the places mentioned and there are some interesting old buildings to visit.

The towns of Bridgwater and Crowcombe are in Somerset and are signposted. Shervage Wood lies beside the road that runs from Bridgwater to Minehead. The map will show you its position. The wood is not far from the sea and is an excellent place for a picnic. Bilberries can still be found there.

Further inland lies Crowcombe, more of a village than a town, and here the fourteenth century church is well worth visiting. The most interesting features, from the dragon hunter's point of view, are its carved pews. Often the carvings on bench ends show religious themes. These are quite unusual as there is nothing Christian about them. Two are of particular interest. The sketch of a bench end in this chapter shows one of them. Here a dragon, with an extra head on its chest, is being poked by two men with poles in their hands. At the bottom of the carving is another dragon's head with a grape vine growing out of its mouth. The other pew shows an enlargement of the dragon's head and grape vine. Here is a fertility dragon!

Two more places are mentioned in connection with the Gurt Vurm. When he was cut in two,

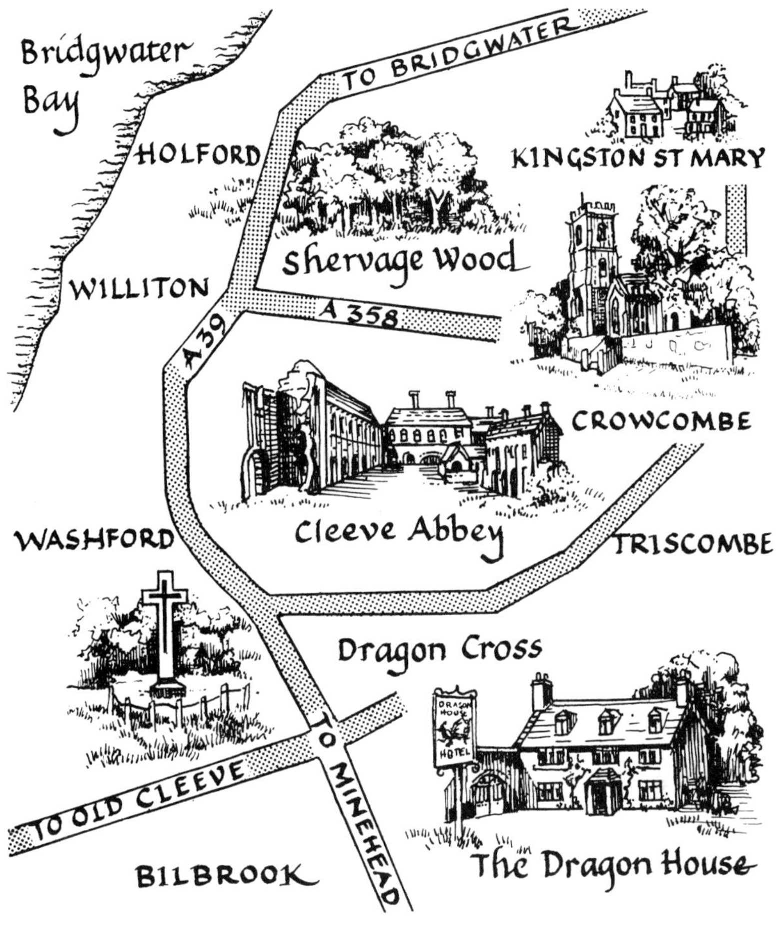

one half went to Kingston St Mary and the other to Bilbrook. The dragon could certainly move when the occasion demanded it, for Bilbrook is quite a distance from Shervage Wood and here again we come across draconian connections. At the Dragon's Cross at Bilbrook, which is the meeting point of three parishes, is a hotel called

'The Dragon's House'. We asked the proprietor why it had this name. He gave us two reasons and both are interesting. It seems that a few years ago the Dragon's House was being extensively renovated. During the course of the builder's excavations, the remains of an old dragon prowed boat were found. It is not known whether this was an actual ship or just a model.

The other reason concerns nearby Cleeve Abbey. In the distant past the building where the Dragon's House now stands was a hospice for pilgrims who intended to visit the Abbey. They would gather together here and walk ceremoniously in file, two by two, across the fields to Cleeve Abbey and their procession would resemble the great coils of a serpent.

A visit to Cleeve Abbey seemed to us the next logical step to take. The Abbey belongs to the Department of the Environment and is open to the public. Although it was built in the twelfth century much of it is in good repair and here in the painted chamber are yet more dragons. The east wall is entirely covered by a late fifteenth century wall painting. This features St Margaret standing on her dragon and at one end of a bridge, in the middle of the mural, stands a horned dragon facing an elderly man with his hands joined together in prayer.

There is one last place to investigate – Kingston St Mary – and here is another legend about a dragon-killing hero. He was an unnamed local lad who was able to kill the dragon without the aid of any conventional weapons. He lured the dragon to the bottom of a steep hill and threw a rock down from the top into its open jaws, choking it to death.

Could this dragon have been the other end of the Gurt Vurm of Shervage Wood? It is quite probable, as the Gurt Vurm's route seems to be one that is well marked in the Quantock Hills.

Carved benchend from Crowcombe Church

5
The Battle of the Barrel

Maud lived with her mother and father in the heart of the country in a small village called Mordiford. It was a peaceful place where nothing much ever happened and Maud's parents allowed her to roam freely in the surrounding countryside. They were sure that there was nothing that could harm their little daughter.

Maud loved all wild animals and often used to take scraps of food with her when she went rambling so that she could feed them. She had even persuaded a squirrel to eat out of her hand. One fine autumn day Maud's mother sent her to pick some blackberries in Haugh Wood. Maud set out with her bag of scraps and some milk in case she became thirsty. The sun was warm and Maud was getting tired of picking berries when she noticed a small creature sleeping among the leaves in one of the bushes. She had never seen an animal like this before. It rested curled up and sparkled in the sunlight so much that it looked as if it was covered with jewels. The little animal's body was no bigger than a cucumber and was coloured grass green.

Maud was enchanted and put out her hand to touch it. This disturbed the creature and it glided up into the air on translucent wings. 'Oh! Come back,' cried Maud in distress and the little flier, seeing that she meant it no harm, alighted on her outstretched hand. She soon found out that, although it rejected her scraps of food, it would drink milk and greedily drunk all that she had brought with her. Maud was delighted with her new pet. She popped him in her pocket, picked up her basket of berries and returned home not knowing that she had found a baby dragon!

'Look, Father,' she said that evening, 'I have found this pretty animal in the woods.' Her father was suspicious of the dragonet. He didn't know what kind of animal it was but he felt instinctively that it could be dangerous.

'You are not to keep that animal,' he told Maud. 'Take it back and leave it where you found it.'

Maud had never feared any bird or beast in her life and could not understand her father's reaction to this one. As she didn't fear her father either she decided to disobey him and keep her

pet where he wouldn't find it. She built a cage for the little creature and hid it in the shrubbery at the end of her garden. Every day she brought it milk to drink and it grew bigger and bigger and bigger.

Soon milk was no longer enough to feed the dragonet for it was speedily growing into a dragon. It broke out of its cage and escaped into the countryside. There it began to catch and eat rabbits and other small animals. But it was growing all the time and before long only an animal as large as a sheep would satisfy its ravenous appetite. Then its eye alighted on the small, plump shepherd boy who was in charge of the sheep. Would he make a satisfying meal? The dragon winged silently above the unsuspecting lad who was sitting absent-mindedly chewing a blade of grass. The dragon's great claws whipped down killing the boy instantly. The shepherd was good to eat. In fact he was so tasty that the dragon decided that, from now on, it would eat human beings whenever it could.

After that no one who lived in Mordiford or the surrounding areas was safe. The dragon attacked men, women and children. The only person that it spared was Maud. The dragon remembered that she had been kind to it and made no attempt to kill her. But now she was as frightened of the monster as everyone else and bitterly regretted that she had not followed her father's advice.

The villagers sought desperately for some way to rid themselves of the murderous creature but no one was brave enough to fight the dragon. There was one exception. In the local prison a condemned criminal named Garston was awaiting execution.

'I will kill the dragon for you if I am allowed to

go free,' he said. The villagers did not have any other choice and accepted his offer.

Now Garston was a wiley and cunning villain and he thought of a scheme to outwit the dragon. He obtained a barrel large enough to hide inside. He then stuck sharp knives and hooks through the body of the barrel from the inside so that the outside bristled like the spiked coat of a porcupine. He was now ready to attack the monster.

Every day the dragon would stalk through the village down Serpent Lane to the River Lugg and quench its thirst there. Garston knew its route and lay in wait, concealed inside the barrel. After a while the dragon arrived and looked at the barrel in amazement.

Then Garston put his plan into operation. He rolled the barrel forward and prodded the dragon with his porcupine spikes. The dragon roared with rage.

'This barrel must have a man inside,' it thought. 'I can smell him. How dare he poke at me!' and it threw itself upon the barrel attempting to break the wood into splinters. But the barrel held firm and withstood the pressure as the monster coiled itself around it. In his rage the dragon had not noticed that the barrel was studded with spikes and the tighter it coiled about the barrel, the more the spikes pierced its body. When it attempted to pull away, the hooks held it firm.

It was not long before the dragon weakened and lay dying, its body cut through and through.

Then Garston slid out of his protecting barrel and cut off the dragon's head. Unfortunately the last few breaths of the dragon sprayed poison into the air and Garston fell dead beside his slain enemy. The villagers rejoiced that they were now free of the fearful dragon and gave Garston a hero's funeral. Maud never again brought home any wild animals that she saw in the woods.

There is not a great deal left to see at Mordiford to remind us of this dragon legend, but this was not always the case. At one time there was a painting of a twelve foot high dragon on the outer wall of Mordiford church. It was erased in 1810 and has never been repainted. It was described in the seventeenth century as an exact copy of the dragon killed by Garston and showed a serpent with four pairs of wings and an inscription which read:-

This is the true effigy of that strange
Prodigious monster which our woods did range.
In Eastwood it by Garston's hands was slain,
A truth which old mythologists maintain.

This portrait had undergone many repaintings and changes during its existence. The dragon has been described as a large green creature with a red mouth and forked tongue and also as a completely red one with a sharply turned up tail. Not long before the painting was destroyed it was coloured green and gold with a long body, legs and wings. It is a pity that this picture can no longer be seen. Perhaps one day it will be repainted.

Lugg and serpent are names associated with the Worm form of the dragon. It is difficult to know which path is Serpent Lane as the streets are not named but you cannot miss the river Lugg which winds in great serpentine loops at one end of Mordiford village. In some versions of the legend the dragon actually lived in the river.

There have been two attempts to try and explain the origins of this legend. It has been suggested that the Mordiford dragon was actually a band of marauding Welshmen who periodically raided the locality. Mordiford is not far from the borders of Wales and the Welsh raiders would naturally be identified with a dragon as this is the symbol on the Welsh flag. The battle between the hero and the dragon would have been the dramatized description of a fight between the Welsh with their dragon banner and the local inhabitants under the leadership of the hero Garston.

It has also been discovered that there was a family named Garston living in Mordiford. They were not low class criminals but landowners with their own crest which was that of a wyvern – a dragon. The painting on the church wall could have been a memorial to a member of the family or a tribute to the valour of one of them in battle. It could even have been a tribute to the valour of a member of the Garston family who was thought to have died fighting a dragon.

Decoration from a Chinese pot

6
Dragon's Retreat

In earlier times St Leonard's forest was part of the primeval forest of Ardenda which covered a large area of Southern England. The Venerable Bede, a learned monk, described it as a thick and inaccessible greenwood which was the home of large herds of deer, wolves and savage boars.

It was in this lonely and dangerous place that there lived an extremely fierce dragon. It was so terrible that tales concerning its violent behaviour were circulated far and wide. Rumours about this dragon were even heard by St Leonard, the patron saint of prisoners and blacksmiths, who lived in a hermitage near Limoges in France.

When this saint heard about the vicious beast and the misery that it was causing in the surrounding countryside, he decided to destroy it and establish his own monastery in the forest. He set out across the channel in search of the monster and was soon hunting the dragon in the depths of the dark woodland. At last, after many days of fruitless searching, he heard the dragon snuffling and snarling as it tore apart the body of a rabbit that it had just killed.

The saint clutched his crucifix to give him courage and attacked his deadly adversary. He fought valiantly even though the dragon's sharp teeth and claws inflicted many deep cuts on his body causing his blood to flow freely on the ground. The dragon was protected by its skin which was hard and scaly and as tough as a breastplate on a suit of armour, but it was no match for St Leonard. The saint forced the monster to retreat through the thick undergrowth, over streams and swampy ground and finally out of the forest. St Leonard was so weak from loss of blood that he was unable to pursue his enemy any further and collapsed exhausted on to the ground. The dragon escaped and the saint never saw it again.

Meanwhile, in the forest, the path that the saint took could be clearly seen for wherever his blood fell on the ground there grew great clumps of lily-of-the-valley. Their delicate scent perfumed all the area.

St Leonard was asked what reward he would like for his brave action in driving the dragon

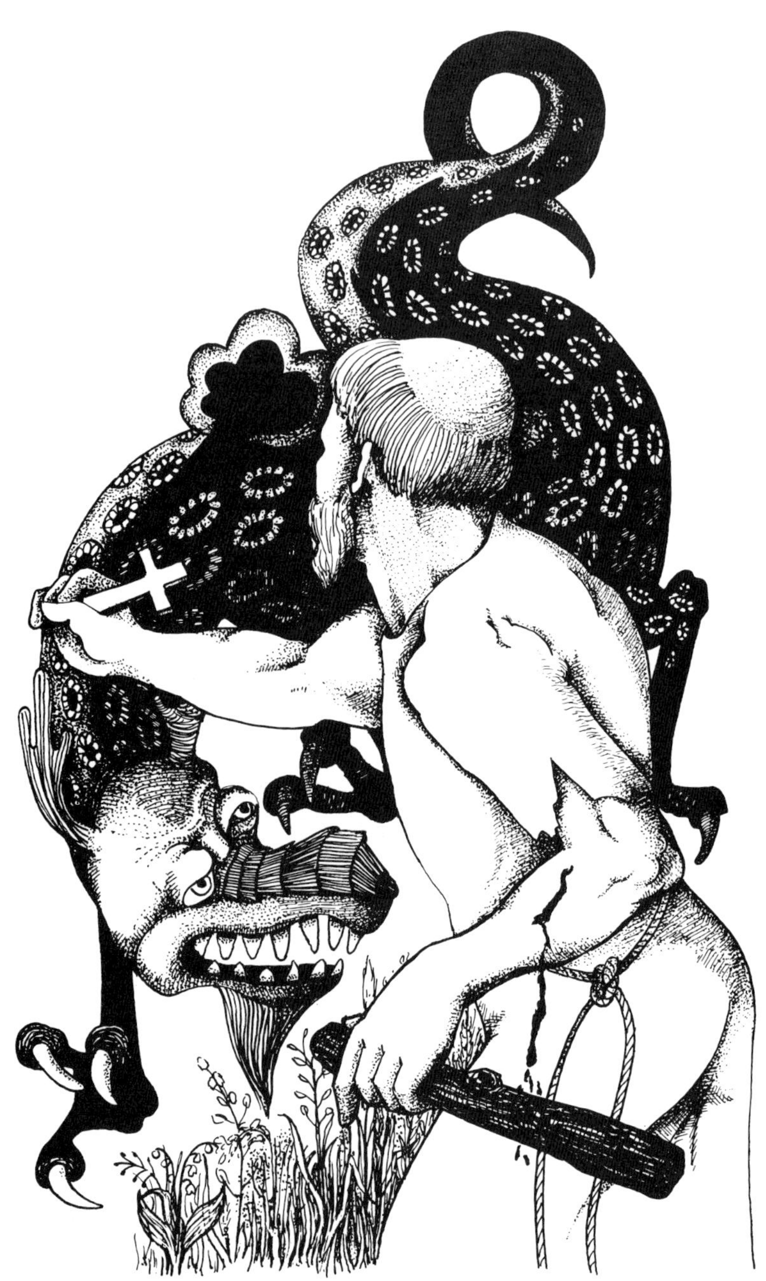

away. He replied that he wanted the eternal silence of the nightingale for its sweet singing disturbed his prayers. This was granted and it was said of the forest that in it:-

The adders never styngе
Nor ye nightingales synge.

The forest remained peaceful until the seventeenth century and then another dragon appeared in the forest. Three people saw it clearly. These three, two men and a woman who lived at Faygate, were lucky to escape with their lives for this creature was extremely poisonous. However, they survived and were able to report their frightening experience to a local printer who published their account of the strange happenings in the forest.

The dragon was described as being about nine feet long with a body that was slightly thicker in the middle than at the ends. Around its neck was a ring of white scales while those on its back were black, its belly was red and the creature carried itself on large feet. On either side of its body were two large lumps, each as large as a football, which looked as though eventually they might grow into wings. The dragon was very proud and when it saw or heard men or animals, it lifted up its head and looked around with great arrogance.

Behind it, in its tracks, it left a slimy, sticky trail rather like that left by a snail. The spoor had a horrible, offensive smell which was thought to be as poisonous as the dragon's breath for it could spit out its venom for a distance of sixty-six feet (that is twenty-two metres).

Some people were not as fortunate as the three from Faygate. A man and a woman were returning home through the forest when the dragon saw them and sprayed them with its poison. When their bodies were recovered they were found to be swollen with venom but not mutilated. Another man bravely set out with his two mastiff dogs to chase away the great creature but it killed the dogs and the man barely escaped. The dragon did not eat the dogs and it was thought that it fed upon rabbits that it caught from a nearby warren.

This was the last time the dragon was seen in the woodland. Perhaps its bulging sides actually grew into wings and it was able to fly away to a less populated area.

The forest is now much smaller than it would have been in earlier times but it is still impressive with its great old trees and hammer ponds. These ponds had been created when local blacksmiths dug there to extract iron-ore (a gift, maybe, from St Leonard who was their patron saint). Part of the forest is known as the 'Lily

Beds' because so many lilies-of-the-valley grow there. It is easy to imagine that a dragon once lived in this enchanting place and a public house on the edge of the forest called 'The Dragon Inn' makes sure that he is not forgotten.

In the legend of the battle between St Leonard and the dragon, the various references to lilies-of-the-valley, dragons and nightingales show that this part of the story is likely to have been an allegory. An allegory is a narrative with another, often true, story concealed under its surface meaning. The lily-of-the-valley is the symbol of the coming of Christ while the dragon and the nightingale could represent a pagan religion. This part of the legend could therefore be interpreted as the eviction of a group of pagans from the forest by militant Christians.

The pamphlet that told the story of the seventeenth century dragon had the exceedingly long title of *'True and Wonderful. A discourse relating to a strange and monstrous Serpent (or Dragon) lately discovered and yet living, to the great Annoyance and divers Slaughters of both Men and Cattell, by his strong and violent poison: in Sussex two miles from Horsham, in a woode called St Leonard's Forest, and thirtie miles from London, this present month of August, 1614.'*

There were a number of theories put forward to try to explain this account of a dragon. Some thought that the creature was an exotic wild beast or serpent that had escaped from captivity. Others thought that the rumours about a dragon were started when the remains of a prehistoric

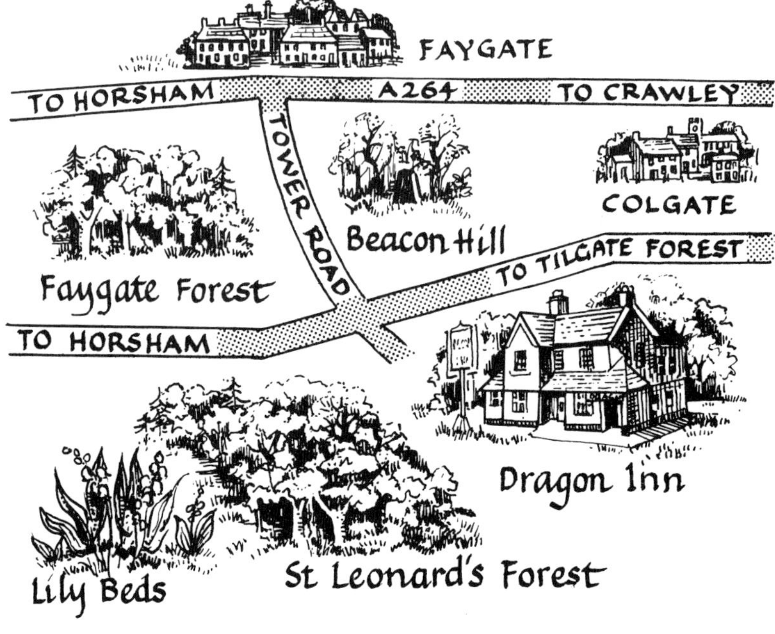

monster were discovered in nearby Tilgate Wood. The pamphlet was considered by many to be a practical joke. If it was fiction, it was practical fiction and certainly not a joke. Stories of supernatural happenings in the forest were encouraged in the seventeenth century because this woodland was the haunt of smugglers. The ingenious smugglers circulated tales of ghosts and fairies who haunted the hammer ponds. Travellers were kept away from the forest by stories of a devil who lived deep in the heart of the woodland and the pamphlet could have been written to frighten away any other inquisitive visitors. The smugglers would have based their story on the ancient legend of St Leonard and the dragon.

Whether the dragon was fact, fiction, misinterpretation or illusion nobody knows. Rumours about the dragon continued until well into the last century. Today there are no dragons in St Leonard's forest unless, of course, you have visited the area and know better!

Letter from a 16th century manuscript

Bamburgh Castle and the 'Bamburgh beast'

7
THE LAIDLY WORM OF SPINDLESTONE HEUGH

BAMBURGH CASTLE was the ancient royal residence of the Northumbrian kings and stands on the harsh and rocky coastline near the holy island of Lindisfarne. In the sixth century A.D. it was the home of King Ida and his two children. The King was lonely and unhappy as his wife had just died and his son, the Childe of Wynd, was abroad fighting the Gauls. He had only his young daughter Margaret to keep him company.

Ida decided that the only thing that he could do was to travel to distant lands to search for another bride. He left Margaret in charge of his great castle and journeyed far away to the wild countries of the West.

Many fair damsels attempted to attract the king's interest but he paid no heed to any of them, for they reminded him too much of his lost wife. However Ida was a rich and powerful king and an evil sorceress determined to secure him and his possessions for herself. She wove her spells of enchantment around the king until the fascinated monarch could think of nothing but her dark beauty and was completely captivated. King Ida married the bewitching sorceress and returned home in triumph with his bride.

Margaret was delighted that her father was home again and after dressing herself in her best gown and jewels ran out to greet her new stepmother. With a shy smile she welcomed the queen to her new home and dutifully presented her with the keys of the castle. The young girl looked so beautiful that all who saw her were lost in admiration. One of the knights in attendance on the queen exclaimed out loud that Margaret was the most lovely creature that he had ever seen.

'You might have excluded me!' the queen muttered angrily under her breath, and from that moment Margaret's fate was sealed for her stepmother had become violently jealous of the gentle princess. The witch-queen concealed her spite behind a smiling face and an affectionate manner for she did not want anyone to guess that she meant to harm the princess.

That night the queen retired to a room high up in the castle and by the aid of her dark powers laid a curse upon Margaret.

'A laidly (loathsome) worm thou shalt be and a laidly worm thou shalt remain until thy brother Wynd returns to Bamburgh,' conjured the queen who was certain that the prince had been killed in battle.

The spell worked and, at daybreak, when her maids went to rouse the princess, they found a great ugly worm curled up in the middle of Margaret's bed. The maids fled shrieking in fright, giving the fearsome creature a chance to slip away into the surrounding countryside.

The worm made her lair in a cave among the crags at an isolated place called Spindlestone Heugh. Although she was now a loathsome worm, Margaret still remembered her previous existence and tried not to destroy the people and places that she had once loved. This was almost impossible because her breath was so poisonous that the land was laid waste for miles around. No one could live there and no plants could grow in such a contaminated atmosphere.

The villagers filled a trough every day with the milk of seven cows, for her to drink. This tribute kept the creature in one place and prevented her from doing further harm. Soon the news of the Laidly Worm of Spindlestone Heugh and the havoc that she caused in the surrounding countryside reached the warrior Prince of Wynd. The lad was determined to free his people from so fearsome a monster and together with his thirty-three retainers made preparations to return home. They built a ship of well seasoned wood with masts made of the rowan tree and hoisted fluttering sails of scarlet silk upon them. It was a magical boat in more than just appearance.

The prince and his crew set off in their fine

ship and the wind blew them speedily over the water until, at length, Childe Wynd saw a high square tower perched on the rocky cliffs. The prince recognized his home and turned his craft towards the shore but such a striking looking vessel was sure to have been noticed.

The queen was looking out of a window at the top of the tower and saw the scarlet sailed boat. She guessed immediately that the prince travelled in it and summoned her evil companions the 'witch wives' to her.

'Cast your spells,' she commanded them. 'Raise a storm and destroy that red sailed ship and her crew!'

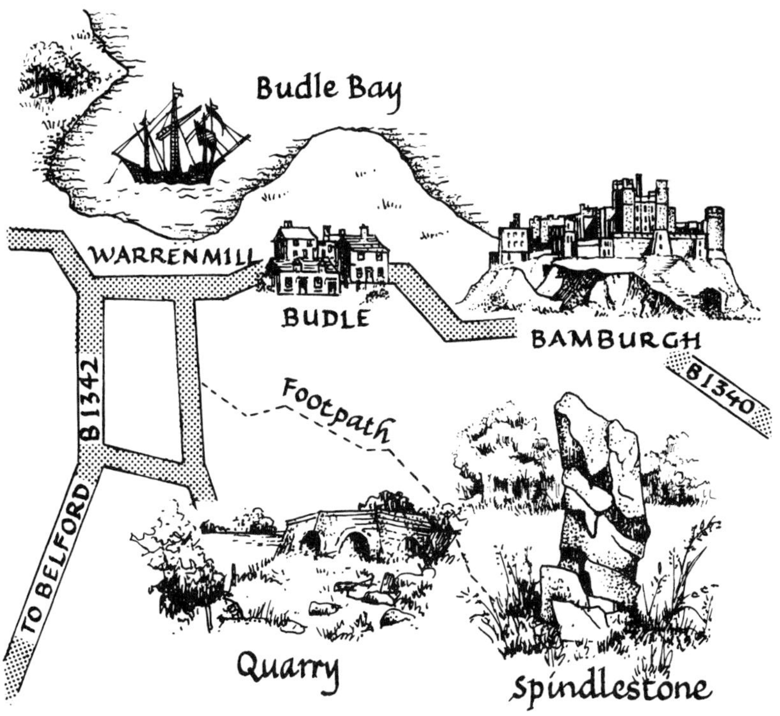

The witch wives recited every incantation that they knew but their spells would not work for the evil was counteracted by the rowan wood of the ship's masts. The rowan or witch tree has magical properties and no evil spirit can prevail against even a branch of it. The queen saw that the witch wives' spells were useless and ordered out a man-of-war to go and destroy the prince's vessel. Fortunately the prince and his men were doughty fighters. It was not long before the queen's ship was scuppered and sent to the bottom of the sea.

Then the worm herself feared her brother's approach and stood on the cliff top lashing the sea into a frenzy with her tail. Her fiery breath drove the prince's boat away from the shore and he was forced to anchor in nearby Budle Bay. Here he borrowed a horse from a neighbouring squire and set off in pursuit of the deadly worm.

The Laidly Worm had retreated to her lair at Spindlestone Heugh and there, coiled around her favourite rock, she waited for the prince to come.

It was not long before the Childe of Wynd found her. He drew his sword and boldly strode towards the monster seeking to kill her at once. The worm lowered her head in surrender and with her eyes full of tears said in a small sweet voice:-

O quit thy sword, unbend thy bow,
And give me kisses three
For though I be a poisonous Worme,
No harm I'll do to thee.

The Prince was amazed to hear the worm speak but did not flinch at having to kiss that hideous visage. He bent forward and gently placed his lips upon her forehead and kissed the worm three times. The worm wriggled swiftly back into her cave where her scales fell off and her gigantic carcass withered away to reveal the princess as beautiful as she had been before the enchantment had been placed upon her.

The Prince of Wynd covered her with his mantle and carried her back to the castle. Her father was overjoyed to see Margaret again. He had been inconsolable because of her loss but unable to do anything to help his daughter because the queen had absolute power over him.

The queen realized that Childe Wynd had triumphed and fled to her bed chamber but she could not escape the wrath of the prince. He dragged her forth and, using the magical powers of a rowan twig, turned the queen's evil spells back upon herself. Before the inmates of the castle could realize what was happening, the queen shrivelled and shrank until she had become a large warty toad crouching on the floor and spitting in fury at the prince. It is said that she can still be seen in the grounds of Bamburgh Castle, transformed into a toad, and spitting at any fair maiden who happens to cross her path.

Bamburgh Castle was built during the reign of King Henry II to defend the Northumbrian coast against northern invaders. It is said traditionally to be Sir Launcelot's castle of Joyous Garde. Today it can be visited by anyone who goes to Bamburgh as it has been extensively rebuilt and is open to the public. The castle stands on a high mound on the edge of a cliff and the outline of it is shown in the illustration at the beginning of this chapter. Also in the picture is a curious headless figure. It is a piece of Anglo-Saxon decoration less than four centimetres long and was discovered during the rebuilding of the castle. It is known as the 'Bamburgh Beast'.

Inside the castle is a romantic painting of the legend surrounded by an illuminated script that tells one version of the tale of the Laidly Worm. The only difference between that story and the one told here is that Childe Wynd was not Margaret's brother but an unknown knight who, in the end, married her.

The rock around which the dragon coiled, the Spindlestone, can be found at Spindlestone Heugh. It is sometimes known as the Bridlestone as it is supposed to be the place where Childe Wynd tied his horse when he advanced to slay the dragon. The dragon's feeding trough and cave have disappeared, and a quarry now marks the place where they once stood. The map shows all these places and the best way to reach them.

The verse quoted in the legend was written by the Reverend Lamb who claimed that he had copied the story from a ballad written in 1270 by

Nereid and a sea monster from an ancient Greek bowl

a singer called Duncan Frazer. Many people think that the vicar wrote the verses himself.

There has been one attempt to try and find the origins of this legend. There was an account written in 1653 by the Laird of Mow about the remains of a sea monster left by the tide on the beach at Bamburgh.

A great roaring and a fearful noise was heard out at sea at Bamburgh and for two years the local fishermen had been unable to catch any fish. At the high spring tide a dead creature was cast ashore on to the beach below the castle. It was the size of a man and had horns on its head, webbed hands and feet, red eyes in a shapeless face and a great tail that hung down to the ground. The smell of the creature soon drove everyone away but not before most folk in the area had seen the sea devil.

Could this story have inspired someone to write the legend about the Laidly Worm? Some people think so but it is difficult to believe that such a romantic tale could have been based upon a hunk of revolting debris thrown up by the sea. In fact the story of a dragon who changed into a noble lady when it was kissed was well known. Can you find any other versions of it? Some of the books mentioned in the book list on page 109 will help you.

Medieval fighting dragons

8
Merlin and the Fighting Dragons

Many hundreds of years ago there ruled a wise king whose name was Lludd. He tried hard to ensure that his subjects lived happy and contented lives but, unfortunately, he was not always successful for his country was upset by three great misfortunes.

The first was that the soldiers of an enemy king, who lived nearby, were always seeking to invade his country. These people practised witchcraft and were able to hear anything that Lludd or his commanders said. Because of this they were always able to defeat Lludd's army.

The second was the disappearance of all the food in the king's castle if it was left out overnight.

The third was a shriek of agony that echoed across the country every May Eve. This sound terrified everyone who heard it. Lludd was upset that these catastrophies were disturbing his people and sought the advice of his brother Llefelys, the King of France.

'The first and second misfortunes are easy to overcome,' Llefelys said. 'Here is a magic powder. Sprinkle it over your enemies and they will soon be dead. When your food disappears, it is being eaten by a giant. Lie in wait for him with your soldiers and when he comes chase him away with drawn swords. You will find that he is easily frightened!'

The third misfortune was more complicated. King Llefelys explained that the scream was caused by one of a pair of fighting dragons.

'A foreign dragon is attacking your national dragon who screams in agony when he is wounded,' he told Lludd. 'Here is the way to solve your problem. Take a silk cloth and spread it over a tub of ale. The dragons will come and rest on the silk, fall into the ale and drink it. Soon they will sink into a drunken stupor and it will be easy to lock them into a stone chest and bury it in a safe place.'

Lludd did as his brother advised and buried the chest containing the dragons in the safest place that he could find. This was on the top of Dinas Emrys, a small round hill that nestled

Merlin and Vortigern from a 13th century manuscript

under the great slopes of Mount Snowdon in Wales.

Five hundred years later, when everyone had forgotten where the dragons were buried, another ruler, King Vortigern, decided that he would build a castle fortress on the summit of Dinas Emrys. It was a good place for a fortress which would protect the entrance to the valley and the lake beyond.

Vortigern designed a magnificent building with towers, barred gates and threatening battlements. It would be completely impregnable. The king put his serfs to work constructing the foundations but they were soon in trouble. The fortress proved to be impossible to build for as soon as the workmen raised a wall, it collapsed back upon itself.

The king was furious and commanded his wisest advisers to solve the puzzling construction problem. He threatened to kill them with his own hands if they failed. The wise men, quaking in their shoes, consulted their oracles, cast their spells and prophesied that, to save the fortress, the king would have to sacrifice a child and bury its body beneath the walls. Not just any child would do! It had to be a child who had not had a human being for its father.

This seemingly impossible task did not stop Vortigern. He immediately organized a search for such a child and sent messengers to every part of his kingdom. After hunting for many months the king's men came across a boy called Merlin living in the depths of a forest. He had the reputation of having a nun for his mother and the devil for his father.

The king decided that this boy fulfilled the conditions of the prophecy and commanded that Merlin should be brought before him. The boy showed no fear as he stood before the monarch and made a brave attempt to save himself.

'Do not kill me,' he pleaded, 'I can save your fortress. I know why the walls keep sinking.'

'Tell me!' commanded the king.

'Dig beneath the foundations,' said Merlin, 'and there you will find two dragons fighting in an underground lake. They are shaking the walls and causing them to fall.'

The workmen dug a great hole in the ground and sure enough, there were two dragons fighting in the muddy waters. One was red and the other was white. As Vortigern watched, the red dragon eventually drove away the white one and emerged victorious from the contest. The king was amazed and immediately rewarded Merlin with the position of his chief adviser. Merlin, in later years, was to become the friend and counsellor of the great King Arthur Pendragon.

This legend is based on actual history. King Vortigern, who lived in the fifth century, was the most powerful of the British kings of that period. He was the king who brought the Saxons to Britain to fight on his side against the Scots, Picts and Roman Britons. This was to prove a very bad policy for eventually the Saxons became so strong that they were able to challenge the armies of Vortigern himself.

The story of the fighting red and white dragons probably describes the actual battle

The fortress at Dinas Emrys

between the forces of the British king and the Saxons. When armies went into battle it was the custom for each side to group beneath a standard showing a dragon of an identifying colour. In this battle the red dragon would represent the British army and the white one would identify the Saxons. In the legend the red dragon – the British – overcame the white dragon – the Saxons – and this, in fact, they did after the death of Vortigern.

The legend of the fighting dragons is Welsh and it is appropriate that a red dragon on a green and white ground is the national flag of Wales. It is said that this story is the reason why the Welsh people adopted the emblem of a red dragon.

Dinas Emrys can be found, as in the legend, at the foot of Mount Snowdon. Excavations were made at the top of this hill in the mid 1950s and some interesting finds were made. First the remains of a twelfth century castle were discovered. Further digging revealed a number of scraps of pottery and ornaments from which it was possible to discover that a number of people lived here in fairly luxurious surroundings during the time that Vortigern reigned in Britain. In the centre of the summit a small depression was found in the ground. When it was cleared out the hollow was found to be a stone cistern. This is thought to have been constructed during the Roman occupation before Vortigern came to the throne.

The dragon on the Welsh flag

Dinas Emrys can be seen from the road near Beddgelert with lake Dinas lying at its foot. Behind them towers Mount Snowdon. If you want to see the countryside where Vortigern ruled, take a walk up Snowdon. The view from the top is fantastic but make sure that you are accompanied by an adult. Climbing this mountain can be dangerous in bad weather.

9
THE WELLS OF THE INVISIBLE DRAGON

IN A WOOD in Longwitton near the village of Thurston there are three wells. The water that is drawn from them has great healing powers and is said to be as sweet as wine. In olden times, many people would visit the wells to try and obtain cures for their ailments. Sometimes a farmer would come there with his aching back or a young woman would seek to ease her sickness by drinking the invigorating water. The Longwitton wells were so famous that people from near and far would come in summer and picnic by the side of them.

One day a ploughman, who was returning wearily home from work, decided that he would visit the wells and get a refreshing drink. Imagine his dismay when he saw a great dragon standing there, lapping up the water with its dark and scaly tongue.

The dragon heard the man approaching and quick as lightning, it made itself invisible. The terrified ploughman knew that it was still there for he could see dead leaves rustling on the ground moved by the dragon's feet. A wind came gusting through the wood. It swirled the leaves around the dragon and outlined its shape as it crouched beneath the trees ready to spring. The ploughman turned and fled, feeling the dragon's hot breath scorching his back as it pursued him to the edge of the wood.

After that nobody was able to visit the healing wells for the dragon had decided to make its home there and would not allow anyone near. Most of the time it remained invisible but everyone knew that it was still on guard. Its tongue could be heard lapping the water, branches were broken from the trees and its claws gouged out great grooves in the ground. One man who actually saw the dragon described it as a huge monster with a warty skin and a long tail.

The people were in despair for there was no longer any cure for their ailments. The ploughman had to put up with his lumbago and the poor old woman who daily bathed her feet there was slowly going lame. They could not think of a way to remove the dragon from the wells.

Help was at hand for the villagers, however, for a knight came riding to Longwitton in search of adventure. This knight had fallen in love with the Earl of Warwick's lovely daughter Felice, who had promised to marry him if he would show his love for her by going out into the world and performing noble and heroic deeds. The knight's name was Guy of Warwick. Guy had heard of the Longwitton dragon and offered to

kill the jealous guardian of the wells.

'Take care, Sire,' said the local squire, 'this dragon has the power to make itself invisible. You will not be able to see where to strike the beast.'

Guy was not dismayed. 'I can overcome that difficulty,' he said, 'for I have a magic ointment which was given to me as a reward for killing another monster. If I rub it on my eyes I will be

able to see the dragon even though it is invisible to everyone else. I will stay with you tonight and fight the dragon tomorrow!'

The next morning he anointed his eyes with the cream and, mounted on his fine charger, made his way to the wood. The dragon was furious at being disturbed. It cast its spell of invisiblity around itself and waited for the horse and rider to come in sight. The knight arrived at the wells and the dragon, who thought that it couldn't be seen, charged at him, striking out wildly with its sharp claws. Guy was ready and plunged his sword deep into the monster's side. It shrieked in agony and retreated to the wells where it stood guarding them but still ready to fight in spite of its wound.

Guy and the dragon battled all day long and the knight inflicted some dreadful wounds upon the monster, but the creature still retained its vigour for its cuts healed almost immediately. Guy was a nimble and efficient warrior but by evening he was completely exhausted and had just enough strength left to ride back to the village. He was ashamed to admit to the squire that he had failed but promised to go and fight the dragon again the following day.

The next day the same thing happened. Guy struck the dragon and wounded it and again its wounds healed and it was as strong as ever. Once more Guy had to retire with his arms so tired that he was unable to lift his sword.

'I will try again tomorrow,' he said to himself, 'and see if I can discover why it is that the dragon can heal itself so quickly. I will use my eyes more and my sword arm less.'

Guy returned to the wells for the third time and continued his battle with the dragon. But now, as he cut and thrust at the monster, he watched it carefully. It soon became obvious that the dragon always kept the tip of its tail immersed in the water of one of the wells.

'Ah ha!' Guy muttered, 'so that is where it gets its strength. I must lure it away from that water.'

He dismounted from his horse, tied it to a tree and attacked the dragon on foot. After a short while Guy pretended that his strength was fading and retreated step by step away from the wells, encouraging the dragon to follow and kill him.

The dragon was deluded into thinking that the knight was beaten and gleefully charged at Guy ready to swallow him up. This was what Guy had been waiting for and he quickly ran round the dragon and placed himself between it and the wells. The dragon saw that it had been tricked and roared like a mad bull as it desperately tried to get back to its former position. But it was too late, for Guy was now able to control the battle and inflicted a lethal blow upon his adversary. Blood poured out of the dragon's gaping wound, burning the ground beneath it. The dragon's eyes glazed over and it fell dead upon the ground.

The local people rejoiced that they were again able to use the healing wells. They spent the next day tidying up the wood and everyone for twenty miles around came to the wells to celebrate and thank the valiant knight.

Dragon hunters will soon become familiar with the fact that a slight legend has sometimes been built around some very notable artefacts and a good story, like this one, can show very little in the way of interesting sites. There is very little to see at Longwitton, only the wells. These have been known as Our Lady's Wells, The Holy Wells or Thurston Wells. The water contains chalybete, sulphur and alumine which give the wells their reputation for healing.

Guy of Warwick was a legendary hero who is said to have ended his days as a hermit. Guy was credited with many noble deeds. He killed the Wild Dun Cow, a monster eighteen feet (six metres) long and twelve feet (four metres) tall on Dunsmere Heath, a savage boar whose head weighed over a hundred pounds (fifty kilos) and another dragon who was about to devour a lion. Soon after he married his sweetheart Felice, her father died and Guy became Earl of Warwick.

As far as it is known no one has attempted to find out why this legend was written. The only site in the area that gives a clue to a possible explanation is the Roman road that can be found very close to the wells. Could one of the religions practised by the road builders have had any connection with this tale? Perhaps they took over the wells as a sanctuary in which to worship one of their healing gods and refused the local people access to them. Two gods, both associated with wells and healing, are obvious choices. They are Mercury and Cernunnos. Cernunnos was also accompanied by his ram headed serpent which is, in fact, a dragon.

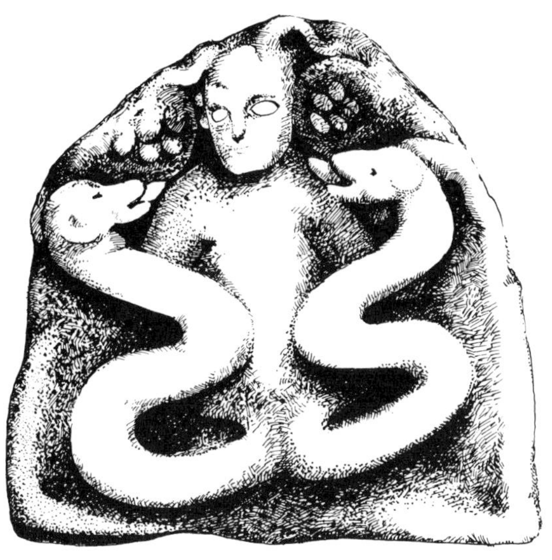

Cernunnos. Stonecarving from Cirencester, Gloucester. The god's ram/serpent companion is duplicated and shown as the actual legs of the deity.

10
The Wyvern of Cynwch Lake

Where it came from nobody knew, but a great wyvern once lived in Cynwch Lake, terrifying the local people and devastating the surrounding countryside. It was a fearsome snakelike creature that could sometimes be seen humping its great coiling body over the fertile slopes of Mount Offrwm leaving a slimy trail behind it. Its venomous tracks poisoned the plants and soil leaving the mount as barren and rugged as it is today.

It didn't matter if it was daytime or night, no living creature was safe if the wyvern was abroad. At night the monster would unfold its wings which, although not large, would beat the air powerfully and noiselessly as it flew about in search of food. The wyvern's keen and penetrating eyes enabled it to see in the dark and its victim, a sheep or an unsuspecting traveller, would hear nothing until the monster's soft, slimy folds closed around him. A terrified scream, quickly silenced, would tell that the wyvern had claimed another victim.

In the daylight the wyvern did not even have to catch its victims for it possessed a strange power over other living things. If another creature looked into the wyvern's glittering emerald eyes, it was doomed. The wyvern would hypnotize its victim and lure it into its greedy mouth. If the prey was too large to swallow, it would drag the carcass to a tree and crush it against the tree's trunk. When the body was crushed to a pulp, the monster would slowly mouth the goodness from the raw meat and lick up any spilt blood with its long, whitish tongue.

It was no wonder that the people were terrified. Local landowners offered great rewards to anyone who was able to kill the evil creature. The Lord of Nannau pledged to give a herd of sixty cattle to anyone who could give him the dragon's tongue.

These rewards tempted Llwyd, the cunning grey wizard of Gallwyd, who decided to make a bold bid to kill the wyvern. Wales has long been known for the accuracy of its archers and Llwyd hired a dozen of the best that he could find. He positioned them around the lake and on the high points of Mount Offrwm with orders to shoot the wyvern on sight. Yet they saw nothing; the creature seemed to sense that they were waiting for it and remained hidden in the lake, concealed by the overhanging roots of rotting trees and clumps of rank vegetation. So the wizard's plan came to nought and he returned home disappointed but vowed that he would frame other cunning schemes to kill the wyvern for he dearly wanted the rich prizes that were offered.

A youth called Mereddith was staying with some shepherds in a valley at the end of the glen. Mereddith was not yet twenty-one years old but he was a strong and sturdy lad who could hold his own in the wrestling ring and had killed a savage wolf by tearing its mouth apart with his bare hands. He hated the wyvern and wanted to kill it not just for the reward (although none would be so stupid as to refuse it) but because of the misery that it caused to his friends.

The youth told nobody of his ambition to kill the monster but decided that he would seek the help of the monks who lived at the Monastery of the Standard, two miles away. He blew the horn at the monastery gate and asked to see the abbot, the wise and saintly old Aneurin. The abbot took one look at the lad's face and did not need to ask why Mereddith had come to visit him. The youth's determination was clearly written there and Aneurin guessed that Mereddith was resolved to kill the wyvern.

Mereddith dropped on his knees before the priest and said: 'My friend, you know the thoughts that I keep locked in my heart. I go on a quest and need the axe carved with the mystic

runes that you keep beneath your altar.'

This axe was believed to have fallen from Heaven and had been found long ago stuck quivering in the oaken door of the monastery. The abbot did not hesitate and placed the weapon in Mereddith's hands.

'Go, my son,' he said. 'Our prayers go with you for I know that you go upon an errand of mercy.'

Near Cynwch lake, Mereddith came across the slimy traces of the wyvern and started following its tracks. Concealing himself behind rocks and bushes, the youth was able to come right up to the monster. It lay coiled up upon the shores of the lake, sunning itself, drunk with the perfume of the may-blossoms that flowered upon a nearby hedgerow.

The stench of the beast almost overcame the brave lad as he crept up to it but his resolve did not waver. He rose up to his full height and swung the sharp axe down upon the wyvern's neck with all his strength.

The severed head fell at his feet but Mereddith was still in peril. The headless body began to writhe in its death throes and its tail struck the lad with cruel force and knocked him senseless.

Some time later Mereddith regained consciousness and, raising himself, saw the dead body of the wyvern lying beside the lake. He felt sick and dizzy but was able to pull himself to his feet and cut out the wyvern's tongue to prove that the monster was dead. He dragged himself back to the monastery, carrying the tongue and the axe, feeling hot one moment and cold the next. He was only just alive for the wyvern's poison had entered his body as he lay unconscious by the lake and it was slowly killing him.

The monks were well versed in the knowledge of medicinal herbs and put all their energies to work in an effort to save Mereddith. They watched carefully over the lad and were at last able to bring him out of his fever.

Then the people all around rejoiced that their dragon-killing hero had recovered. Mereddith was given the cattle and many other valuable gifts and from then on he was no longer a humble peasant boy but could take his place among the great and noble people of the district.

The only person who was not pleased was the wizard. How could he claim any reward now that the wyvern was dead? He tried to obtain his revenge by bewitching Ellyw, Mereddith's sweetheart, causing her to lose her way in a treacherous bog, but even in this he failed. Mereddith went out looking for her and she was found before it was too late.

Mereddith and Ellyw returned home to his parents at Halford where they were married. As is usual for dragon-killers, the wyvern appeared on the coat of arms of Mereddith's descendants together with a shepherd's crook and an axe.

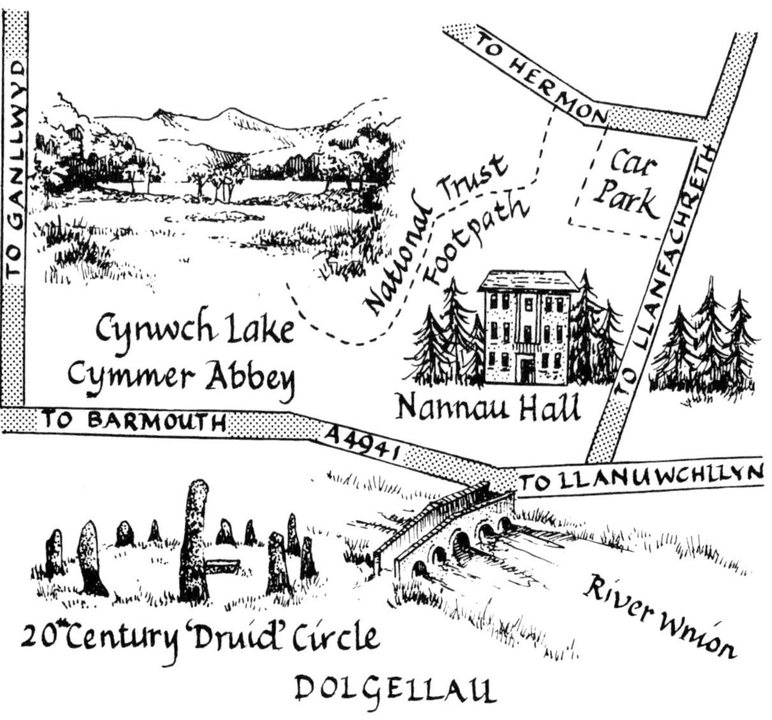

It is easy to visit Cynwch lake because it is part of a nature trail. The map shows the route and there is a car park close to the path. Mount Cynwch slopes down to the water on one side of the lake and there are thick woods on the opposite shore. Nowadays sheep graze peacefully close to the water's edge. It is said that Cymmer Abbey near Dolgellau is the place that was called the Monastery of the Standard in the legend.

Cynch Lake is a mile long stretch of water. It is difficult to imagine its calm surface concealing the threatening shape of a lake monster. However, this legend should be compared with other legends concerning lake monsters like those in Loch Ness and Loch Morar. Apart from the statement that it can fly, the wyvern shows a remarkable resemblance to these creatures. It has humps, was seen on the slopes of a hillside adjacent to the lake and could not be spotted when a search, by a number of people, was in progress.

Maybe the legend of the Wyvern of Cynwch Lake was based upon the finding of such a creature in the lake. The story would naturally be embellished with a lot of bloodthirsty details and the creature was presumably killed.

The dragon-killer was certainly no conservationist. It is to be hoped that should another lake monster surface from the lake, turning out to be a dragon in the flesh and not just a fabulous beast, it will be met with only cameras and not the traditional iron weapon.

Wyvern from a 12th century bestiary

The dying dragon at Martin's stone which is decorated with pictish designs

11
THE LEGEND OF NINE TEMPTING MAIDENS

NEAR DUNDEE , in Scotland, is a village called Pitempton. Here an old crofter and his nine daughters lived together in a small cottage. The youngest daughter was only seven but some of the older girls were of marriageable age. One was betrothed to a young farmer named Martin who dearly loved his gentle sweetheart.

One Sunday evening in winter, the old man and his daughters were sitting around the fire when the father discovered that there was no water in the pitcher on the table. He turned to his youngest daughter Bridget.

'Go to the well,' he commanded her, 'and fetch me some water to mix with my whisky.'

The little girl did not protest although she had been warm and comfortable by the glowing fire; she put on her cloak and went out of the door and down the path that led to the well.

The father waited and waited for his drink but his little daughter did not appear. He turned crossly to another girl.

'Go after Bridget,' he said. 'Hurry her up and bring me my water!'

The second sister went in search of the youngster but she didn't return either. The old man became increasingly annoyed and turned to another of his daughters.

'Those two are fooling around out there,' he exclaimed. 'Find them and make them hurry up.'

The third girl also rose and went in search of the other two and when she didn't return he sent four more of his daughters, one after the other, in search of them. The two remaining girls became very worried and apprehensive. The eldest, Martin's fiancée, whispered to the other:

'Meg, I am going to see if I can find our sisters. Perhaps a wild animal has scared them away from the house. I will take some food and try to lure it away so that they can return home.'

'Be careful,' said Meg who was by now feeling extremely frightened.

She waited by the door and tried to see if she

could catch even a glimpse of her other sisters but it was too dark outside. She could hear the soft sound of the elder girl's feet on the path, then silence and the faint call of a nightbird. Or was it a cry for help from her brave sister? Meg did not stop even to pick up a coat but ran swiftly down the path to the well. A horrifying sight met her eyes! In the pallid light of the partly obscured moon a gigantic dragon with gleaming scales the colour of burnished copper was coiled around the base of the well. Its tail was wrapped around her sister who stood shaking with fear, unable to escape. Worse still, the dragon's mouth was wide open as it held another girl between its fangs. Meg turned to flee but it was too late, the dragon had seen her. It hastily swallowed the dainty morsel in its mouth and struck out at the running girl. The last thing that its unfortunate victim saw was its glittering eyes as it swept her up in its jaws.

Back home at the cottage, the old father was also very worried and fearful. At first light he ventured out and could see in the distance the great dragon coiled around the well protecting it. There was no sign of his daughters; he had unwittingly sacrificed them all to the dragon.

Blinded by tears, the old man stumbled to the farm of his late daughter's sweetheart Martin and told him how his nine daughters had died. Martin was heartbroken. He felt as if there was nothing left to live for and he no longer cared if he lived or died. The only emotion, besides grief, that he felt was hatred for the pitiless creature

who had killed the defenceless girls. He took up his cudgel and set off in search of the dragon, resolved to kill it in revenge for the deaths of his bride-to-be and her sisters.

The dragon saw the brawny lad coming and uncoiled its great length from around the well. 'It will be harder to kill a strong man than it was to slay those delicate girls,' thought the dragon as it slithered away. It dragged its long body over the ground and through a morass at Baldragon in an effort to escape, but it had eaten nine girls and the weight of all this food made it slow and sleepy. By the time the dragon had reached Strathmartine, Martin was close behind it and, raising his heavy club, he dealt it a frightful blow on the head.

The dragon writhed in agony and slithered away as quickly as it could through the undergrowth but it didn't get very far. Martin caught up with the monster as it squirmed across a cornfield and followed up his attack. After the enraged lad had struck a few dozen more hefty blows, the dragon lay dying. It raised its head up on to a stone that lay in the middle of the field and with blood pouring from its mouth, choked out its dying speech:-

I was tempit at Pitempton,
Draiglet (dragged) at Baldragon,
Striken at Strikemartine,
And killed at Martinstane.

This was the end of the dragon and the stone still stands to mark the spot where it died.

All the places mentioned in the verse can be visited. The map on page 98 shows their position in relation to Dundee, the nearest town. The Nine Maidens Well is now filled in, only a slab remaining to show where it once existed. There is now a public house in Pitempton called 'The Nine Maidens'. The next places on the map are Baldragon which translates as 'the homestead of the dragon' and Baldragon Wood. Then comes Strathmartine (in the verse it was spelt Strikemartine as this is the way that it was pronounced by local people). Martin's stone lies in a field two miles north of Pitempton. This three foot tall stone is the broken base of a Pictish cross and the front of it is covered with decorations. The faint outlines of horses and riders can be seen together with an animal that archaeologists describe as an elephant because it has a protuberence on its head. At the base of the stone is a fat serpent lying across a zig-zag line. It would be interesting to see if this stone marked part of a ley line perhaps aligned to the site of the Nine Maidens Well.

It is likely that this legend was tailored to fit in with a series of village names to make an amus-

ing rhyme. However, the significant part of it has no connection with the place names. That is, nine maidens sacrificed to a dragon who guarded a well. The legend could be the remembrance of a pagan religion whose fertility rites included human sacrifice or which took the villagers' daughters away to serve their gods.

Maybe the dragon was a form of meteorological phenomenon. From the earliest times, the dragon was associated, in people's minds, with elemental forces like rain, floods and thunderstorms. In the past there have been reports in north-east Scotland of red lights in the sky called 'Fiery Drakes', followed by strong winds and boisterous weather. The foul weather could have included a thunderbolt or lightning strike which killed all the members of a household, and the story of the misfortune might have been handed down to us in the form of this dramatic legend.

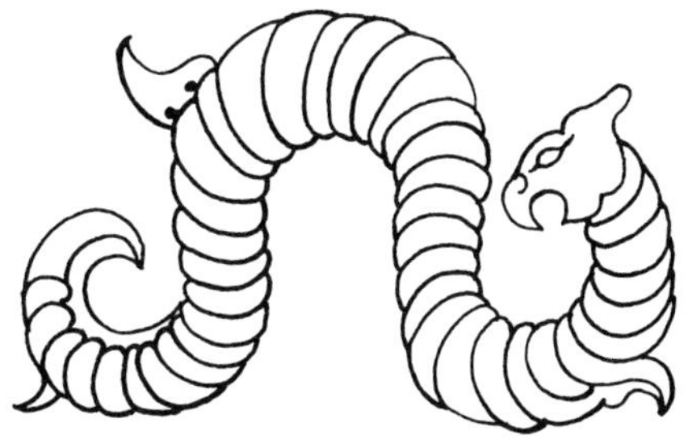

Jade Chinese dragon

The white horse of Uffington

12
WHO WAS ST GEORGE?

To save a mayd St George the dragon slew,
A pretty tale if all is told be true.
Most say there are no dragons, and tis sayd
There was no George; Pray God there was a mayd.

AUBREY

THERE ARE many wondrous sights to be seen in the lands of the East but not all of them are safe to look at and some are quite deadly. The dragon who lived in a lake near the city of Silene was one such phenomenon. It was a giant creature with a gleaming golden hide; beautiful on the outside, within it was more poisonous than the most deadly rattlesnake.

It would have caused very little harm if it had stayed in the desert but it had once tasted animal flesh and now came right up to the city gates in order to obtain another helping of this delicacy. When it found the gates closed against it, the evil creature killed many of the citizens of Silene by blowing a cloud of its poisonous breath over the walls.

Naturally the rest of the citizens were horrified. Each day they killed two sheep and left them some distance away from the city walls as an offering to the beast. This satisfied the voracious creature and it did not come up to the city walls again. Unfortunately the supply of sheep and cattle could not last for ever and the day came when the inhabitants of Silene were unable to find any more food to give the dragon. What could the people do to protect themselves?

The king called his citizens to a meeting and a law was passed that each day two of their own children would be offered up to the dragon. The victims were chosen by lot and every day a sorrowing parent would have to bring his son or daughter to be eaten by the dragon. No one was spared!

After many of the inhabitants of the city had lost their children, it happened that the lot was drawn by the king's gentle young daughter Sabra. The king was crushed by despair.

'Take my gold, my silver, half my kingdom,' he cried, 'but spare my daughter.' But the people who had sacrificed their own children to the monster demanded that the king should follow their example. The maiden was dressed in her finest clothes and jewels and led out of the city. Her sorrowing parents remained in the castle for they could not bear to see their young daughter face such a frightful death.

As the princess stood weeping by the side of the lake she was observed by George, a knight from Cappodocia who was passing that way.

'Why are you crying?' he asked her.

'Good knight, mount your horse and leave this area or you will die with me,' she replied. George would not do as she asked.

'Why are you so frightened?' he persisted. 'What fate awaits you here at the lakeside?'

The maiden tried to persuade him to depart. 'Please go,' she pleaded, but George stubbornly refused to leave as he was sure that the princess would die if he was not there to protect her.

At this moment the dragon rose to the surface of the lake shaking pearly drops of water from its awesome gleaming skin. Still the young girl, trembling in fear, urged the knight to go. George's only answer was to make the sign of the cross, commend himself to God, take up his lance and advance to meet the monster.

The dragon opened its gaping mouth wide in order to swallow this foolhardy adventurer but George cast his lance into its mouth with such force that the point penetrated through the dragon's throat and pinned it to the ground. The dragon lay with its head in the dust completely overcome.

The knight turned to the maiden and said,

St George from a 17th century Ethiopian manuscript

'Fear nothing. Take your girdle and pass it round the neck of the dragon. You will then be able to lead it back to the city.'

The girl did as he requested and the dragon followed her like a docile dog. The population fled at the approach of their hateful enemy but George told them not to be afraid.

'The Lord sent me to deliver the princess and you from the dragon. Priase his name for it is He that has delivered this enemy into your hands.'

Then the king and all his people, over twenty thousand souls, were baptized and George smote off the head of the dragon.

The chief source of this story is a book called *The Golden Legend* which was written in the thirteenth century. *The Golden Legend* recounts the stories of the imaginary lives of a number of saints. Writers, in olden times, would compose these fictional biographies of saints to act as morality tales showing good triumphant over evil, like the stories of, say, Superman today. They were written to amuse their readers and to teach them good behaviour. *The Golden Legend* was a work of fiction and St George, along with a number of other saints, must also be regarded as fictional. The Catholic Church certainly thinks so, for in 1960 the Vatican declared that St George was no longer a saint.

However some fictional characters are based upon actual people and there is, at least, one man who could have been the person upon whom the character of St George was founded. He is reputed to have been born in Lydda and was martyred around A.D. 300 for protesting against the Emperor Diocletian's decree against the Christians. The martyred body of the saint was returned home to be buried in Lydda near the town of Joppa and an interesting piece of information can be found concerning this locality. At Joppa is an offshore rock where Perseus was said to have slain a dragon to save the

Princess Andromeda. The bones of this monster were exhibited in the city for many years. You can read this legend in the Greek myths. The stories of St George and Sabra and Perseus and Andromeda are nearly identical. It seems likely that this exciting myth of a princess and a dragon was grafted on to the sober story of a martyred saint to make it more interesting. Like some other Christian saints St George was credited with the deeds and legends of an earlier hero.

But what has this got to do with British dragons? In the twelfth century English knights were setting forth on crusades to the Holy Land. A warrior would naturally be interested in the story of a saint who was also a courageous knight and the legend of St George became popular with the crusaders who eventually returned to England with the story.

Not only was St George popular with the Crusaders but soon he became well known throughout England. Farming communities also identified him with their own fertility spirit, Green George. It was not long before people started claiming that George had killed the dragon in their own particular part of the country. There are two places in England that are said to be the exact spot where the dragon died. One is in Wiltshire and the other is in Herefordshire.

High on the hillside, straddling the downs above the Vale of the White Horse in Wiltshire, a great chalk figure can be seen cut into the earth. This effigy has been known as the White Horse of Uffington for the last 900 years. Just below the figure is a low conical shaped hill which is known as Dragon Hill. This is one of the places where St George is said to have slain the dragon. The poisonous blood of the creature, spilt as he lay dying, caused a bare patch on the top of the hill. Even today there is hardly any grass on the top of Dragon Hill. In Saxon times King Cedric and his warriors are supposed to have slain the Pendragon Naud and his army of 5000 men on this hill. Perhaps that is how it got its name.

Dragon lore is so popular in the White Horse Vale that some people consider that the chalk figure is not a horse at all but a dragon. It certainly looks like one as it has a beaked jaw and a long thin body that ends in a tail. Whether it was meant to be a horse or a dragon it is impossible to say. As it is so old it is more likely to have been a horse, as a dragon would have been drawn with a more wormlike shape. Whatever it is, the graceful form of the White Horse of Uffington harmonizes beautifully with the hills and valleys that surround it.

The other place that is claimed to be the spot where the dragon was killed is totally different. This dragon, who lived at Brinsop in Herefordshire, was yet another dragon who lived in a well, this time in Duck's Pool Meadow. St George fought and killed the dragon in a nearby field called Lower Stanks. Here again is a bare patch of ground where the dragon is supposed to have died. The next village is called Wormsley.

North of Duck's Pool Meadow is Brinsop Church. Here is another reminder of St George for built into one of the church's inner walls are the remains of a twelfth century tympanum. This sculpture shows St George killing the dragon. The saint's face is missing. The tympanum was probably one of the religious sculptures that Cromwell damaged during the Civil War. In spite of this it is a powerful carving, eerie and ominous. The church stands within the raised circle of an old earthwork, and both it and the surrounding area seem charged with a curious power. It would be easy, here, to imagine a doom laden worm gliding through the undergrowth, rustling old dry leaves as it slithers over the ground.

12th century tympanum from Brinsop Church

Book List

Folklore

The book of Imaginary Beings. J. L. Borges, 1980

The Fairies in Tradition and Literature. K. M. Briggs, 1967

The Greek Myths. R. Graves, first printed 1955

Folktales of the Northern Counties. F. Grice, 1944

Wonder Tales of Ancient Wales. B. Henderson & S. Jones, 1921

Folklore of the Northern Counties of England and the Borders. W. Henderson, 1973

Saints in Folklore. C. Hole, 1966

English Fairy Tales and *More English Fairy Tales*. Collected and retold by J. Jacobs, 1890, 1894

Fabulous Beasts. B. P. Lum, 1952

British Dragons. J. Simpson, 1980

The Lambton Worm. P. Screeton, 1978

Folklore, Myths and Legends. Readers Digest Publications, 1977

Dictionaries

Dictionary of Fabulous Beasts. R. Barber & A. Riches, 1975

Dictionary of British Folktales, Part B. K. M. Briggs, 1971

Colour Books

The Flight of Dragons. P. Dickinson, 1979

Dragons. P. Hogarth & V. Clery, 1979

The Dragon. F. Huxley, 1979

All Colour Book of Biblical Myths and Mysteries. G. Thurlow, 1974

General information

Animal Fakes and Frauds. P. Dance, 1975

The Ley Hunter's Companion. P. Devereux & I. Thompson, 1979

The Dragon. Charles Gould; ed. Malcolm Smith, 1977

Signposts to the Past. M. Gelling, 1978

Complete Guide to Heraldry. A. C. Fox Davies (various editions)